Swami Chinmayananda

First Edition	November	1995	5000	copies
Second Edition	August	1996	5000	copies
Third Edition	November	1999	5000	copies
Forth Edition	June	2001	5000	copies
Reprint upto	February	2008	20,000	copies
Revised Edition	May	2010	5000	copies

Published by:
CENTRAL CHINMAYA MISSION TRUST
Sandeepany Sadhanalaya
Saki Vihar Road, Mumbai - 400 072, India
Tel. : (+91-22) 2857 2367 / 2857 5806
Fax : (+91-22) 2857 3065
E-mail: ccmtpublications@chinmayamission.com
Website: www.chinmayamission.com

Distribution Centre in USA:
CHINMAYA MISSION WEST
Publications Division
560 Bridgetown Pike, Langhorne, PA 19053, USA
Tel. : (215) 396-0390 Fax : (215) 396-9710
E-mail: publications@chinmaya.org
Website: www.chinmayapublications.org

Printed by:
Thomson Press (India) Limited
Thane-Belapur Road, Airoli, Navi Mumbai - 400708, India

Price: Rs. 120.00

ISBN: 9788175974869

1st January

There is no New Year
that I know of.
We,
with our mind's
passions and hopes,
conceive
the coming year
and the year
that has gone off.

2nd January

Rest in Him
who is ever the same
in your heart
and
watch the parade
of events
in the stream
of time.

3rd January

A man
firmly established
in freedom is tranquil.
His equipoise
is never broken,
even when he is
investing his entire energies
on the world outside
for the service of mankind.

4th January

You must
be ready to
accept
all things
as
natural,
with quiet
cheer.

5th January

Do not believe
it possible
to
be wedded
to
worldly life
and yet
be an
ascetic.

6th January

The tragedy of
human history is
decreasing happiness
in the midst of
increasing comfort.

7th January

A man of
integrity
is accepted,
believed,
trusted and
befriended
by all.

8th January

A well trained

and

controlled mind

stands

a man in good stead,

better than armies.

It saves him

from cowardice

as well as perils.

9th January

The cultured
give
happiness
wherever
they go;
the uncultured,
whenever
they go!

10th January

The spirit of
advaita
is not to
keep away
from anything,
but to keep
in tune
with everything.

11th January

Don't put

the key

to

your happiness

in

someone else's

pocket.

12th January

Lives
of great men,
their
deeds and words
always
stimulate
and
ennoble
our
mental life.

13th January

Everybody exists.
It is only the few
who live.
To live,
you should
have an
ideal.

14th January

The greatness is
not in what we do,
but
unavoidably
it is always
in
how
we do
what
we do.

15th January

Fools give up
the loin-cloth
and other externals,
but do not reject that
whose rejection
alone really matters.

16th January

When opportunity
knocks,
we
are either
out
or sleeping
in.

17th January

It takes two
to make a quarrel.
Also it takes two
to make up
after a quarrel.
Without
invoking love,
this can never
be accomplished.

18th January

"End the mind
and remain great"
is the
thunderous bidding
from
every corner
in the Hall
of
Vedānta.

19th January

To give

love

is

true freedom;

to demand

love

is

pure slavery.

20th January

Advaita
is possible
only
in feeling
and not
in action.

21st January

No one,
while steeped in
sensuous pleasures,
can ever find
abidance in
Brahman.
Can lotuses
ever grow on rocks
or hair
on tortoise shells?

22nd January

Continuous
change alone
is the
changeless
law.

23rd January

Death connotes
not only the condition of
the body when life has
ebbed out from it,
but includes
the very principle of
change and finitude.

24th January

The
subject
of dhyāna
must ultimately
come to find
its identity
with the
object
of dhyāna.

25th January

All learned people
admit that the paramount
duty of a sannyāsin
who has renounced
the world
is the uninterrupted practice
of spiritual discipline,
which alone
leads to mokṣa.

26th January

Renunciation is the
only way to perfection.
Even a little
renunciation is rewarded
with immense blessings.
Renounce!
Renounce!!

27th January

Grief
is the state
of mind
created
by the absence
of objects of
one's liking.

28th January

Restlessness of the
mind
and unsteadiness of
character
are reflected
in the
physical movements
of an
intelligent being.

29th January

Who is a friend?
He who
comes to you
with love and cheer
when
all others have left you
is a true friend.

30th January

A true friend
is
discovered
not by searching outside
for a right person
to befriend,
but
by your
growing to be
the right person
to deserve a friend.

31st January

You are never
away from
Him.
You are in
Him, with Him,
at
Him.
You are
Him
alone.

1st February

REFLECT!

<u>Scare:</u>

Young men never care
to listen to advice.
This is their nature.
Nobody needs to curse them for it.
Yet when they
once trip and fall,
they learn for themselves.
A serious scare is always worth
more to a teenager
than any amount of advice.

2nd February

Actions
are the
louder expression
of thought.
The quality
of thought
is ordered
by the nature
of our inner belief
and faith.

3rd February

Any activity
undertaken
by a perfect Master
does not and cannot
bring about any
consequences,
good or evil, upon Him.
He is only
a divine instrument.

4th February

It is a matter of common experience that the knowledge of a subject by itself will not enable a person to act always according to it.

5th February

Meet life
as it reaches you.
With or without the things
our minds demand,
life can be
a brilliant success.
But, for this,
we must discover
something else
to depend upon.
Seek that something
within yourself,
not outside.

6th February

Man becomes
high
or
low
according
to his
deeds.

7th February

The contents
of the present moment,
divorced
from all relationships
with the
past and future,
is the
absolute fullness
of the
Infinite.

8th February

Carefully navigate
around the dangerous rocks
of thy own lower nature.
Thou shall reach
the eternal Heaven
of peace and bliss —
Truth.

9th February

Mind at rest
is the
temple of joy.
So long as
it is gurgling with
its desires, passions
and attachments
in its stormy surface,
the signature of joy
gets ruffled out.

10th February

In life,
the glory lies
not in the quarry,
but in the chase.
The success is
not in the trophy won
but
in the
race run.

11th February

Comfort
comes
as a guest,
lingers
to become
the host,
and stays
to
enslave us.

12th February

To be patient means to suffer something that hinders or hurts us, and still retain our self-composure. How many difficulties, with their consequent unpleasantness and discord, could be smoothed over and almost entirely eliminated by patience. Patience always elevates and strengthens our character. We need patience not only with others, but also with ourselves.

13th February

Man is the
roof and crown of creation.
He may be tossed about by
uncertain storms of life,
but the solution to it lies
in his own efforts
in finding an ideal
and then raising
his personality, from the
level of petty emotions,
to the loftier heights
of the chosen ideal.

14th February

Our present work
may be
great
or
small.
Yet,
the important thing is
to do
it well.

15th February

The Lord
is ever with you.
Your own
anxieties and fears
are veiling
Him from you.
He is so near to you
that you cannot
see Him
You are
in Him — at Him.
You are He alone.

16th February

Even

the

devil

knoweth

not

the

mind

of man.

17th February

You alone are in your heart.
You unconsciously got
locked in and you cry out
to others to open up and
release you. Nobody can.
Stop crying. Find the handle
and turn it... Lo! It has opened,
and you immediately get
a blast of the life-giving,
reviving breeze of fragrant,
cool love from all around.

18th February

Even though
you have not conquered
the battles of the world,
you become
the world-conqueror
when you
have conquered your mind.

19th February

Stop all your
attachments to false values.
In an ever changing world,
there is nothing worthwhile
for us to desire or weep for.
Joys and sorrows
are bound to come
in human life;
they are just like
the two sides of
of the same coin.

20th February

The mighty Himalayas
seem to
symbolize
the Almighty Himself,
and the Ganges
looks as if
she were overflowing
with milk.

21st February

A Brahmātman is one
whose Ātman has
become one with
Brahman;
one who has found his
identity with the Self
everywhere.
He is called
Brahmavid,
the knower of Brahman.

22nd February

The incompetent
and
the ineffectual alone
grumble
that they would have
done much more
had the circumstances
been different.

23rd February

The inward
tremors
are experienced
only when
any burning desire
has conquered us
completely.

24th February

Dignity
of
labour
consists
in
service.

25th February

Efficiency
is the
capacity
to
bring
proficiency
into
expression.

26th February

Equanimity in the
face of life's challenges
must not flow out
from the dark cages of
one's inertia and stupidity;
it must gurgle out
from one's own wisdom
and understanding.

27th February

Charity is an attempt wherein
I try to expand and bring into
the ambit of my life, all others around
me and grow to consider
the other man's needs and requirements
as important as my
own personal needs. To live
seeking an identity thus, with
at least those who are
immediately around me, is to
live away from the suffocating
selfishness and the throttling grip
of my body-consciousness.

28th February

Liberation
or attainment of perfection
is a condition experienced
by the mind;
liberation is
only for the mind
because
the mind alone
was in bondage.

29th February

Man awakened
to the
Self's glory is God.
God,
forgetful
of
His
own true nature
is the deluded man.

1st March

REFLECT!

Faith:

Faith in yourself
and in the goodness of the Supreme
are necessary accessories
for accomplishing all great achievements.
But, mere blind faith is impotent.
It must be followed by sweaty efforts
and panting hours of work.
You accomplish nothing with faith alone,
and you can do nothing without it.
Cultivate faith and support it
with your honest and sincere efforts.

2nd March

Action
includes not only
physical
but also mental actions,
conscious and
subconscious.
Action is, in short,
everything
we think and do.

3rd March

The quality of
activities
cannot be raised
unless
we raise the very texture
of our thoughts
and the depth of
our understanding.

4th March

The knowledge of
Brahman
is the immediate
perception
of non-difference between
Brahman
on the one hand and
the universe
on the other.

5th March

Silently
hear everyone.
Accept
what is good;
reject and forget to
remember
what is bad.
This is the way
to live
intelligently
in life.

6th March

By birth
man does not
become
an outcast
nor does he
become a
high caste man.
He becomes
high or low
according to his
deeds.

7th March

Love
is to
human hearts
what the
sun
is to
flowers!

8th March

Suffering
depends,
not upon the
factual happenings,
but upon the
texture
of each one's mind.

9th March

Some act
till
they meet obstacles;
others act
in spite of obstacles
and conquer them; but
some act not
fearing the possibility
of obstacles
that might arise
enroute.

10th March

Become
quietly effective.
Don't expect "them"
to fully
understand you.
They won't!
So, demonstrate
with results,
what they would
not understand
with words!

11th March

Wisdom is the
assimilated
knowledge in us,
gained from an
intelligent estimation
and close study
of our own
direct and indirect
experience
in the world.

12th March

To train
ourselves
to endure meekly
the little
pinpricks of life
with magnanimous
joy — heat and cold,
pain and pleasure,
success and failure —
is itself the
highest sādhanā.

13th March

A
Man of wisdom
lives in the
world,
but he is
never of the
world.

14th March

Everyone
points to the other man,
who, according to him,
is happier.
But the only one who has the
courage to declare
that he is truly happy
is he who has
relinquished
all his passions and hungers
from within.

15th March

The fiery touch
of the Lord's grace,
when it descends upon
His devotees,
is invariably felt
by the seeker
more as
a refreshing shower of
divine mercy.

16th March

Yoga
is
skill
in
action.

17th March

Not sickness,
but health
is
the mystery
of life.

18th March

Whatever
springs
in the mind —
man
expresses
it.

19th March

Without devotion,
knowledge is tasteless.
Without knowledge,
devotion is mere empty
idol worship.

20th March

Anger
is nothing but an
attachment for an object
when expressed towards
an obstacle
between ourselves
and the object of
our attachment.

21st March

Among men,
he
whose mind
is ever fixed on
Brahman,
is the best and
noblest.

22nd March

Wherever
there is the concept
of the other,
there is
fear, restlessness,
agitation, worry,
anxiety,
each
following the other.

23rd March

Desire
is
at the
root
of
all actions,
good
or
evil.

24th March

Act
efficiently whenever you
work.
The results of action
depend upon
the very
quality of action.

25th March

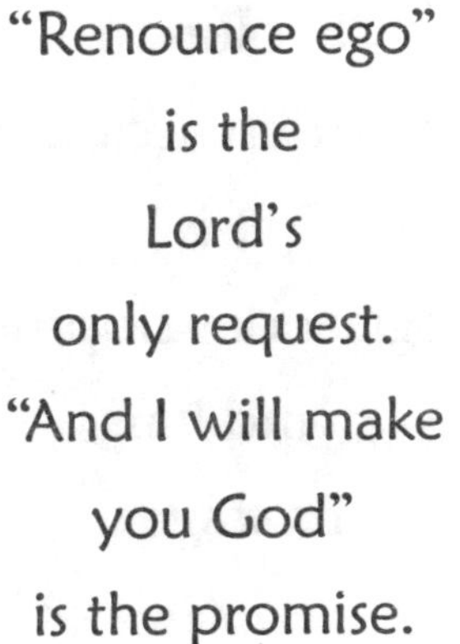

"Renounce ego"
is the
Lord's
only request.
"And I will make
you God"
is the promise.

26th March

Evolution

is not an accident.

It is

a logical development

and has

its stages.

27th March

Work
without faith
and
prayer without sincerity
are like
artificial flowers —
without
fragrance.

28th March

A

quiet mind

produces

a

more

brilliant

intellect.

29th March

Learn
to speak softly
always
words of
love and affection,
then
friends multiply.

30th March

God
is not purchasable
nor is He
available
for one's persuasions
to be an ally
in one's animalistic
activities.

31st March

If
money
does not
bring
happiness,
give
it back.

1st April

REFLECT!
<u>Strive on:</u>
History is full of instances
wherein victory would have been
to the vanquished,
if only they had
battled a little longer!
We often fail
for the lack of perseverance
in our efforts.
We leave our work half done,
in our impatience.
Every job demands
its quota of efforts.
Never give up too soon.
Strive on
until you win!

2nd April

Enthusiasm is the very fuel in all great men. By inexhaustible ardour for whatever they undertake to accomplish, they generate an extraordinary drive for action. In spiritual self-improvement and in serving the nation in its cultural and spiritual aspects, the workers and missionaries must discover within themselves the secret of invoking this trajectory-force of true and flawless enthusiasm.

3rd April

This is
the very call of the Gītā:
"Tasmāt uttiṣṭha kaunteya
yuddhāya kṛta niścayaḥ —
Shed your fear.
Get up, determined to
fight and win!"
Get up my countrymen —
determined to fight,
to die
if need be —
for the sacred Bhārata.

4th April

In the darkness of
ignorance,
we attach ourselves
to the unreal
and the fleeting.
In the light of
knowledge,
we identify ourselves
with the real
and the permanent.

5th April

Have patience
and live in true endeavour
with Īśvara smaraṇa.
The best will
surely turn up.
Now and then,
in everybody's life
comes a small crisis.
Face it bravely.
The Lord
looks after everyone.

6th April

The man
who is not
proud
of his motherland
and who is not
true
to his customary duties
must be regarded as
a base, ungrateful fellow.

7th April

We may
often
give
without love,
but we can
never
love
without giving.

8th April

The quality of
a mind
determines
how the
ego
reacts
to a given challenge.

9th April

Live morality
before you talk about it.
Practice meditation
before you preach it.
Taste goodness
before you recommend it.
Gain bliss
before you offer it
to others.

10th April

Human as we are,
let us never look back
for a moment, but
dynamically march forward,
creating a glorious future of
magnificent achievements by
rightly exercising
the independent self-effort
that is man's prerogative.

11th April

Temper
brings you
trouble.
Pride
keeps you
there!

12th April

Life is full of waves —
pain and pleasure,
gain and loss,
conquest and defeat
must buffet the waters of life.
Otherwise,
it is complete stagnation.
It is death.

13th April

The secret of success,
behind all men of
achievement,
lies in the faculty of
applying their intellect
in all their activities,
without being misled
by any surging
emotions or feelings.
The secret of
success in life lies
in keeping the head above
the storms of the heart.

14th April

In all worthwhile undertakings, there will be risks of failure, of disappointments, of even disaster. To face them all with inner poise and firm faith is to discover the glory of final victory. A conquest without facing dangers is as dull as victory without a shining glory — a game without a prize!

15th April

The greatness in an
ideology is not
in fact in the ideology;
it is
in the subject
who lives
that ideology.

16th April

The secret of action
is to get established
in equanimity,
renouncing
all egocentric attachments
and forgetting to
worry over our successes
and failures.

17th April

At all times,
send our
thoughts of
love to all;
kindness to all;
blessings to all.
Soon you will find
all
including your enemies,
showering you
with love.

18th April

The mind has
to be raised
step by step,
from the gross state
to
the subtle state;
then
to the causal state
and still further to
the great cause, and thus finally
to Samādhi.

19th April

The leisurely moments of contemplation are the occasions when the dreadful mask of nature falls off and we peep into the encouraging, kindly beauty of life and its environments. Thoreau asserts, "When we are unhurried and wise, we perceive that only great and worthy things have any permanent and absolute existence; that petty fears and petty pleasures are but the shadow of the reality."

20th April

Ātman

is

sat-cit-ānanda

as

electricity

is

heat-cold-light.

21st April

The difference
between
Brahman
and the
world of objects
is the lateral inversion.
Consciousness
is infinite;
the world
is finite.

22nd April

Multiplicity
of worldly concerns
binds down a
sannyāsin
as much as any
householder.

23rd April

Conquest
of
desire
is
kaivalya —
the
highest
goal
of man.

24th April

God

is not an

object

to be found

outside.

Stop

searching!

Discover

Him

within.

25th April

The ego,
born
into a suitable
physical body and
living through the
required field of circumstances
gathers the matured
fruits of actions done
in ignorance
and
animalism in the past.

26th April

Running away
from life
is not the way
to reach
the highest goal
of evolution.

27th April

It is but human to make mistakes, to fall prey to some temptation, to get enchanted by some false emotion, or to elope with a wrong intention. But how quickly can one regain his original goodness measures one's spiritual poise acquired. In short, fall often as you must, but don't lie down where you have fallen like a rock. Be yourself, ever like a rubber ball; rebound and pant up to reach again the summit from where you had the fall!

28th April

The

quieter

the

mind,

the

sharper

the

intellect.

29th April

In short,
the ability to love
and express it in action
is the requirement
in gathering
more and more friends.
In fact,
love in action
is the heart of all religions.

30th April

Know
what to do
and then
do it
yourself.

1st May

REFLECT!

<u>Imagination:</u>

Many get enchanted by their own imaginations, dreams and fantasies. There is no harm in these dreams, if one does not believe them to be real and consider them as already gained! All great achievements have sprung from dreams, stemmed forth from imagination, indeed have sprouted up and grown from fantasies, but accomplished through effort, hard work and self-application. Don't imagine your sincerity in work, but work sincerely with imagination. Plan out your work and work out your plans.

"Shed your fear. Get up, determined to fight and win!"

2nd May

Thoughts
in an individual expressed
in the outer world of
objects
become his
actions.

3rd May

The bright
beginning
made each day
can become
the
early dawn of
the day
of achievement.

4th May

It is easy
to develop the
intellect
but it is difficult
to develop the
heart.

5th May

To argue that
life results when
lifeless matter combines
itself,
is as absurd as
holding that
light comes out of
darkness!

6th May

Grief

and

dejection

are the price

that

delusion

demands from

its victim —

man.

7th May

Love
is something
to be
sustained and
fulfilled
by loving.
By loving alone
can love be
made to grow
and thrive.

8th May

Who says I am 70?
Who is 70?
The boy born at
Ernakulam (Kerala) and
named Balakrishnan?
He died in 1943-44.
Then he was born as
Swami Chinmayananda.
Are you celebrating the
Swamiji's 70th or
Balakrishna's 70th?
What folly!
What māyā!

9th May

Swami Chinmayananda is 44 years old! Of these, 36 years I had been doing my pūjā of people as best as I know, day and night, with no Sunday off or casual leave or summer vacations! Life is to be measured not by years but by the quantum of sevā done, with honest and sincere devotion. That way if you consider a 36 years' work to be equivalent to 70 years of life, I do not protest, I just smile!

10th May

To keep the records straight, you must realize that there are different opinions regarding the age of this swāmi. From my correspondence I find people informing me that I am now 71,72,73 and also 74. How can I reply to them honestly? Who can? We all know we were born — but who knows when? It is all hearsay!

11th May

Prayer is not to change
the pattern around you,
but to give you protection
from them.
We do not travel in a boat
to stop waves,
but the sides of the boat
do protect us from the raw,
direct hits of the waves.

12th May

Wrong imagination
is the bane of life.
All failures
can be directly traced to
an impoverished mental
equanimity created by the
unintelligent entertainment of
unfounded fears
of possible failures.

13th May

Plan out your work;
then work out your plan.
The former
without the latter
is a sheer waste.
The latter
without the former
is mere unproductive
confusion.

14th May

When the
sāttvika vāsanās
increase,
your devotion
to your
ideal
grows
more and more.

15th May

As the thoughts,
so the actions.
Immoral thoughts cannot
lead to moral actions. Actively
non-cooperate with the
lower instincts
by immediately
remembering the
Lord.

16th May

Prosperity
is like wine,
which goes to the head
and makes man forget
his Creator.
Adversity
on the contrary
sobers him and
reminds him of
God and His glory.

17th May

This love
that we have
needs constant giving
and as we give away,
it gets replenished from His
Infinite Source.
But if you refuse
to give love,
the stagnant love
in your own heart putrifies
and the crawling worms
start eating up
your own heart!

18th May

In
introspection
the mind
itself
is the
subject
of study.

19th May

Desire, anger
and their numberless
children of sin and sorrow breed
in the marshy lands
of our own
deluded intellect.
To remain
under their sway is
ignorance.
To rule over them is
perfection.

20th May

The outer world can
gain a capacity
to ill-treat man only
when the individual
exposes himself
unguarded.
He is then crushed
by his own attachments
and wrong valuations.

21st May

Whenever
your attention is drawn
towards
the world of objects,
think of
its unreal nature.
The world is nothing
but the reflection of Brahman,
having no reality
apart from it.

22nd May

Intuitive
illumination
occurs
the very instant
when
ignorance
is dispelled.

23rd May

Desire
is called sinful
since
in its grosser expression
it makes us
live and work,
satisfying
our lower nature.
It thus results
in over-living the life of
a lower level of evolution.

24th May

Disappointments
come only to those
who make appointments
with the future.
Do make appointments,
but only with the present.
Then disappointments
can never, never come.

25th May

We suffer silently
wounds
inflicted by weapons;
suffer
the pains of diseases;
yet
to suffer the thought,
"I am not the ego"—
why such dread?

26th May

Each experience
is a perceptible
mental
disturbance (manovṛtti).
The illuminator
of these vṛttis is
the One that lights up
the concept of time
in our lives.

27th May

The vision
of an
indescribable
thing
must necessarily
be
indescribable.

28th May

If the mind
is filled with
sattva,
the other two guṇas
perish
by themselves.

29th May

Friends are made
by many acts
and
friends are lost often
by a single thoughtless act.
You must grow up
to deserve a friend.
To have friends,
you must have
friendliness in you —
be selfless and loving,
with deep concern
for others.

30th May

If you want
to prove
God,
improve yourself.
That is the
only
method.

31st May

He who seeks
happiness outside
himself
will never find
satisfaction.
It is an illusion
to think
that
more comfort
means
more happiness.

1st June

Spiritual unfoldment
cannot take place
merely because of
an intellectual appreciation
of the theory of perfection.
Evolution takes place
only when
a corresponding change
in the subjective life
is accomplished.

2nd June

Actions are
nothing but the
actor's thoughts
projected
and
expressed
in and through
him.

3rd June

To give
without sympathy is to
build a temple
without the idol,
and is as futile as
painting
a picture with black
ink,
on a black board.

4th June

Spiritual
knowledge
cannot
be given;
take it.

5th June

Be regular.
Be sincere.
Make each day a
rounded beauty of love,
goodness and joy.
Live in
the bliss of the
best
thoughts,
said and done.

6th June

A man of
full realization
instinctively
becomes a lover
of the
whole universe.

7th June

Our work is
love made visible.
When love is made
to manifest, work is done.
When we work
only to produce profit
or wages,
work becomes
crushing, sweating,
joyless labour.

8th June

Depersonalization

is the

secret

of

inspiration.

9th June

We are only
instruments in His hands.
Never identify yourself with
your outer personality —
son of so and so,
husband of such and such, etc.
Be ever
a pliant reed
in the hands of
the Eternal Flute Player.

10th June

Character is formed
from the
repeated choice
of thoughts and action.
Make
the right choice;
we shall
have a firm
and
noble character.

11th June

Unless we have
a definite faith in
the goal of our existence
and unless we believe,
work for and
actually come to experience
the goal
positively
as an existent factor,
there is no hope
of any plan
becoming successful.

12th June

A mere detachment
in itself is only
a negative existence of
merely escaping from life.
The perfect one,
ever established in the Supreme,
experiences both
the best and the worst
in life
with equal detachment.

13th June

When
the intellect gets purer,
it will lose
all its present charms
for sense experiences
that it had before or may
gain in the future.

14th June

A successful

man

is one

who

can lay a

firm foundation

with the bricks

that others

throw

at him.

15th June

Everything will straighten
itself in time.
Only we need patience,
faith and self-surrender.
The Lord is great.
He knows best
the purity of
every thought,
action and motive.

16th June

An intellect
fuming with anger
comes to experience
delusion
and the deluded
discrimination
comes to lose
all memories of
the past.

17th June

Cease
to give love,
and we cease
to have love;
this is the strict
law of love.

18th June

To dissipate ourselves
with
immoral and criminal
thoughts is more harmful
than physically
indulging in them.
The mind has a tendency
to repeat its own
thoughts.

19th June

A situation is
judged by the intellect
as honourable or
dishonourable
with reference to
its own existing values
and
cultivated habits
of thinking.

20th June

A plan can
deliver
its promised
blessings
only
when the plan is
executed
with
promptitude.

21st June

The learned man who discountenances the efforts for the realization of Brahman is more dangerous than the ignorant one.

22nd June

You are the mirror
in which
the whole cosmos
is reflected.
How can mirror
complain of the
dancing things
seen in it?

23rd June

Desires are
never
quenched
by enjoyment.
It rather
inflames them,
as
clarified butter
does fire.

24th June

Divine law
does not entitle
everyone to everything.
To attach ourselves
to the Divine
is to detach ourselves
from the un-divine.
To walk into light
is to walk out
of darkness.

25th June

The ending
of ego
is the
realization
of the
supreme
state.

26th June

He who has
experienced the
Higher
refuses to remember and
relive the past.
Even a street dog
will not eat
its own disgorging.

27th June

Whenever there is danger for righteous life, when all norms of dharma are flouted, when lust for power and cruel plunder pass for strength, it is the religious duty of the faithful public and devout rulers to fight the satanic forces with all their might and wisdom. Our religious literature is replete with such righteous wars. The ten avatāras of Viṣṇu are eloquent pictures of Hinduism in action. Why, the very symbol of Viṣṇu speaks volumes for the dynamic Hindu way of life.

28th June

To expose the mind
to the quiet atmosphere
of meditation upon
the All-pervading Being
is to heal
the mind of ulcers
and cause it to
become perfect
in wisdom.

29th June

Love
for
one's equal
is
called
friendship.

30th June

You can
cheat
others,
but never
your
conscience,
Your
God.

1st July

Contentment in
anything that
reaches him accidentally,
unasked and unexpected,
should be the motto of
all serious seekers of
inward growth.

2nd July

The secret of action
is to get
established in equanimity,
renouncing all
egocentric attachments,
and forgetting to
worry
over our
success and failure.

3rd July

Great achievements
are earned
not through
proficiency alone,
but
achievements are
rewards
of
efficiency.

4th July

True knowledge
enables a man to realize
that he is
the soul with a body.
Now, in his ignorance, he thinks
that he is
a body with a soul.

5th July

If
the Infinite were not
conditioned by matter,
It would not be able
to express
Its glories
as vividly
as we see it today
in the multiple universe.

6th July

The ordinary man
gets involved in the
activity
of this world,
but not
the Man of Perfection.

7th July

The Man of Perfection,
even while living
in the physical body
attains infinitude,
though he may be a PFT*
from the standpoint of others.
The Man of Realization
has the attitude,
"though doing,
I am not the doer."

*PFT: Perceiver, Feeler, Thinker

8th July

As your body
requires daily cleansing,
so does
your mind.
So long as
your mind is
full of negative tendencies,
you can never
bring it to
single-pointed concentration.
Control the mind.

9th July

There is no
vessel to ferry
man
across the
ocean of worldliness
except
jnāna.

10th July

One may
change
one's dress easily,
but who can
change
his heart
with the same ease?

11th July

The universe
is a cosmos
and not a chaos.
There exists
a mental affinity,
a scientific law,
a rhythm of mental relationship
in which
the entire living world
is held together
in one web of love.

12th July

The stream of happenings,
come and go irresistibly
around and above you,
and that which gives
the balance to face them
steadily is prayer.

13th July

You are
successful
and
creative
only when
you see
an opportunity
in
every difficulty.

14th July

We compromise with
our ideal
in seeking
the temporary gratification of
some passing whim of
our mind.
On such occasions
the usual justification is
that it is
a necessary evil.

15th July

Love
is the
greatest
persuasive
power
we know
in life.

16th July

Leap from
the shores of duality
into the rugged boat of
discrimination
and ply ceaselessly
towards the
horizon of experience.

17th July

Kṛpā
is an
attitude of sympathy
cooked in kindness,
honeyed with love
and served
on golden platters of
understanding.

18th July

Where
we keep the
mind in peace,
there worry is
not in itself a sin,
but like all sins
it is precious energy
misspent in unproductive
and
wrong directions.

19th July

However much
an individual or a team
of workers, may toil,
a cultural renaissance
cannot come out of it
directly.
A national culture
has its roots in the
individual character;
it thrives and blooms only
on the fertile soil of
our actual behaviour
in life.

20th July

The source
of all
bliss
is the
dedicated
performance
of duty.

21st July

Bondages are
created upon our
personality and life
by none other than
ourselves.
These bondages,
infinite in number,
are produced by
the subtle chord of our attachment
to things.

22nd July

Constant
contemplation
upon
sense objects
is the cause
for
bondage.

23rd July

He who believes
that fall
is antecedent
to rise
will never
give way to
despair.

24th July

Divinity
is not to be given
to you
from somewhere else.
The Upaniṣad
thunders,
"That Thou Art."

25th July

Each embodied life
indicates
a long autobiography of
the ego;
it is only after
a long chain of
existence
in different forms
that it has,
at last,
reached the present
destination.

26th July

We choose
our
joys
and
sorrows
long before
we experience
them.

27th July

Let
the helmsman
be thy śraddhā, and
keep the boat
steadily towards
the Pole Star,
the mahāvākya.

28th July

Doing
good
in return for
evil
is the correct
morality.

29th July

More important
than what is
behind you
and
what is
ahead of you
is what is
in you.
Seek It.
Centered in it,
act and live.

30th July

Man
cannot see
God
but
God
is not
un-experienceable
non-existence.

31st July

Learn
to be happy
alone.
If we do not
enjoy
our own company
why inflict it
on others?

1st August

REFLECT!

Perseverance:

Consistency
in doing anything
has in it
the assurance of success.
This — in a noble cause —
is perseverance.
It becomes obstinacy
in a bad cause.
Both are consistency of effort.
Perseverance is
positive and creative.
Obstinacy is
negative and destructive.
You have the choice
to choose intelligently.

2nd August

Bhakti
is the attitude
of the mind
and
jñāna
is the attitude
of the intellect;
both flow
towards the
Lord.

3rd August

Hindu culture
is essentially based
upon the sacrifice
implied in duty
and not
upon acquisition,
which is
implied in rights.

4th August

All disturbances
and challenges
arise not only from
our relationship
with others
but in
our attitude to
all the other
things and beings.

5th August

Never brood
over things
which have happened,
or worry
over things
yet to happen.
Live in the present.
Intelligently
face life with
a tranquil mind,
full of prayer
and Īśvara smaraṇa.

6th August

The summit of vairāgya
is the
total absence of
desire
to seek any enjoyment
in the
world of objects.

7th August

When our hearts
are full of
love,
life is a
smiling valley of
beauty
and
joy,
romantic
and divine.

8th August

Whatever be the
form of
God,
only a mind
which has freed
itself totally from
worldly entanglements,
can be filled
with
divine love.

9th August

Faith
is to believe in
what you do not see,
the reward
of which is
that you see
what you believed.

10th August

Seek the Lord
in the smiles of
your friends,
in the glow of
angry eyes,
in the storms of
passion.
He is everywhere,
in everything.

11th August

Bhakti
and
service
are
inextricably
connected.

12th August

Just living
the routine life of
unintelligent imitation of
others in society
is the surest way to
a life of sensuality.

13th August

Strange!
Wealth estranges us all.
It is all very strange,
the money psychology!
When you get some,
you grow jealous of others
who have more,
and feel conceited
among those who have less!

14th August

The train runs
but not the steam;
the fan moves
but not the electricity;
the fuel burns
but not the fire.
The body, the mind and
the intellect function
but not the life,
the Self in them.

15th August

Be a
tapasvin
and learn to tap
the very source of
all life and joy,
which is verily
in thyself.
Go inwards
towards the
Lord
in thee.

16th August

We pray for peace
but we shall not yield
to adharma.
We live in contentment
but never shall we submit
to aggression.
We are soft,
but never
when we deal
with naked evil.

17th August

Association
fastens
love,
while
separateness
reduces
it.

18th August

Let
the worldly man
live in
Vārāṇasi or Kailāṣa,
at
Badri or Gaṅgotri.
Wherever he be,
his mind
will be attached
and fickle.

19th August

Active participation and observation are not always necessary to understand and live an experience. Had not da Vinci painted "The Last Supper" without attending it? Why do you try to avoid meditation because you have no experience of it? Meditate! Start today now! Meditate!

20th August

The body
is the same
in the case of
the knower
and
in the case
of the ignorant.

21st August

That which has
neither
a beginning
nor
an end
can have
no cause of
Itself.

22nd August

Indeed, even the
austere
sannyāsins
are
susceptible
to the beauty
of
creation.

23rd August

The action of today
becomes
the destiny of tomorrow.
If after all our efforts,
the vāsanās are
not totally exhausted,
then the balance
that remains to trouble us
is called destiny.
Man can change
his destiny,
not by wishing for it,
but by working for it.

24th August

Let your
hands and legs
function;
but let a part of
your mind
steadily
hold on to
the idea of
the divine essence
in you.

25th August

The attitude of
egolessness
is the secret of
unveiling
the nobler
and
the dynamic
in us.

26th August

A
strong man
is
one
who faces facts.
He is weak
who wants to
escape
from them.

27th August

Be like a
flower.
Give
happiness
and
fragrance
to
all!

28th August

Be a noble person in life.
The tides of circumstances and
the tussle of happenings may
toss us hither and thither,
may buffet us up and down; but
stay noble in your thoughts
and actions and you will be
ever safe.
This nobility in your heart
must shine out in your actions,
in your conduct, in your work.

29th August

Whatever
leads man to God
is acceptable;
whatever
stands in the way
of realizing God
should be rejected
totally and
unceremoniously.

30th August

Love of
God
is the bright sun;
desire for
sensuous pleasure
is
darkness
itself.

31st August

Be free
from the persecution of
both joy and sorrow.
Such a one alone can
find peace here, below.
Live in Him
who is beyond
both these
the Illuminator,
the Ātman.

1st September

REFLECT!

<u>Hope:</u>

Hope is necessary
and can be an inspiration
in living
if it is well controlled
and well disciplined.
Like tamed birds,
we must clip the wings of our hopes,
so that they may
never fly over the fence!
If you hope for
the occurrence of the impossible
in the long run,
such disappointed hopes
may severely embitter your life.

2nd September

When love rises
to swirl around us
and when we review
in this clear light of love
the very faults
get transformed into
the essential beauty
in them.
This is the
magic touch of love,
the miracle
played by love.

3rd September

The real men of
achievement are
people who have the heroism
to fuel
more and more enthusiasm
in their work
when they face
more and more difficulties.

4th September

He
who has
transcended
egoism
experiences
everlasting joy,
finding himself,
Paramātman,
in everything.

5th September

Life is
full of changes.
The faster
the changes,
the faster
we are moving.
See
His hand
in all
changes.

6th September

Man is
subject to such misery
only because
he is disobeying
the law of life
as discovered
and described
in the scriptures.

7th September

Tomorrow
we will be
what we are now,
plus
what and how
we have faced
life's challenges today.
This is the law
of
cosmic justice.

8th September

The world of plurality
has an irresistible charm
to entangle and
ensnare us in
our attachments.
To avoid the ugly stain of
bad vāsanās,
wear the gloves of
constant Īśvara smaraṇa
on your minds.

9th September

We

like

someone

because;

we

love

someone

in spite of.

10th September

Be
ruthlessly
discriminative.
Let not the heart
wander away
without
the intellect,
its
master driver.

11th September

To assume
differences
in the world
is to
belie
this great
oneness
in life.

12th September

Be

openly happy

in the joy of others.

Be

sincerely sympathetic

in others' sorrows.

13th September

Religion
must not be
considered true
because
it is necessary;
but
necessary
because
it is true.

14th September

There is
no companion like
solitude.
The one who knows
how to tune himself to
the inner silence,
even in the midst of
the din and roar of
the marketplace,
enjoys
a most recreative
solitiude.

15th September

Things happening
around us are interpreted
by our mind
and we label them
and come to experience
them as great tragedies
or wonderful blessings.

16th September

How
can the limited mind
comprehend the
formless
and
unlimited
Brahman?

17th September

The one
in love
expands
to function
from two points —
from oneself
and
from one's
own beloved.

18th September

Mind
cannot
contemplate
on any theme
that cannot be
conditioned
by the
senses.

19th September

If

I dislike you intensely,

then

even if I see you

performing a good deed,

I label

all your actions

as

vile and vicious.

20th September

When

the body is fully relaxed,

consciousness

has retreated

from the body and is

localized

more intensively

in our

mind and intellect arena.

21st September

It is the
theory in philosophy
accepted in
scientific observations also,
that an effect
can only
perish
to become the cause.

22nd September

Indeed,
criticism
is like a
boundless sea.
Once you
get into it,
you can hardly
get out of it.

23rd September

Detachment
from the
world of objects
is never possible
without attaching
ourselves
to something
nobler and divine.

24th September

The divine
in us becomes a friend
when under its influence
the satanic in us
gets converted.
The divine qualities
are the means
and
Godhood
is the end.

25th September

The ego
survives within us
so long as
we entertain
thoughts.

26th September

Do not

live in sentiments.

Live in true intelligence.

Do not yield to

unhealthy attachments,

low thoughts,

vulgar motives.

Be bold

in your faith in Him.

Be bold! Be bold!

27th September

Forgiveness
is an ornament
to men and women alike.
Forgiveness
is the secret beauty
in any spiritual seeker's life.
Not to forgive,
is to maintain the passions
bottled up within us.
Then we are never empty enough to
lift ourselves
in our soaring meditations.

28th September

We cannot
do away
with the shortcomings
in our personality
without
the world,
the body
and the scriptures.

29th September

God's
prasāda or grace
held by whomsoever,
is precious.
God's
grace
is everything,
that
transcends everything.

30th September

To

misunderstand

a man

is easy;

to understand

him

is difficult.

1st October

REFLECT!

Cultivate excellence:

Anybody can win
if he be the sole entry.
Unfortunately, in every field of
human endeavour,
there are many entries.
And so, to win,
one has to cultivate excellence.
The excellent man has
a better chance to win,
than a slipshod, third rate,
careless idler.

2nd October

The God-man
functions
as a true sportsman
in his playfield,
where the enjoyment
is in the very sport
and not in the score.

3rd October

Success

or

achievement

is

not the final goal.

It is the spirit

in which you act

that puts

the seal of beauty

upon your life.

4th October

Consciousness
devoid
of all objects
would be
pure
Consciousness —
pure Knowledge.

5th October

The true service
of a teacher lies in
the attempt of the student
to attune himself
to the principles of life,
advocated and advised
to him
by the Master.

6th October

Man
at any given point,
is
the sum-total
of his thoughts
which he
consciously
entertains.

7th October

Karma,
when undertaken
with no anxiety for
the results,
integrates the personality.
When a heart
is thus purified,
a clearer discriminative
faculty comes
to play through it.

8th October

By mere physical service the total happiness can never come about in the community. The members must develop their spiritual stature through their religious faith and practice. Hence our students should have regular sādhanā of kirtan, bhajan, a bit of Vedic chanting, attending regularly ārati at Śrī Rāma temple, etc.

9th October

Flood your mind
with love.
Look
into the eyes of
the other and
embrace the person
with whom
you have quarrelled.

10th October

In the human heart,
there is
always a great tendency
to glorify one's own
weaknesses with some
convenient divine pose
and angelic name.

11th October

Silently
hear everyone.
Accept what is good.
Reject and forget
what is not.
This is
intelligent living.

12th October

Life,
when properly
tuned
can round
the sharp edges
in our
character.

13th October

Sandalwood perfumes even the axe, that hurls it down! The more we rub sandalwood against a stone, the more its fragrance spreads. Burn it, and it wafts its glory through the entire neighbourhood. Such is the enchanting beauty of forgiveness in life.

14th October

Love is
not love
if it does not
serve
and
sacrifice.

15th October

Desire to possess, when directed towards Nārāyaṇa, becomes the burning spiritual anxiety of devotion for the Lord.

16th October

Mind
can create
beliefs in scores,
dogmas in dozens
and speculations without end.
Mind
can forge God or Gods,
but it cannot unveil
Reality.
The mind must bow and fall
to reach the Self.

17th October

To have as much
love of God
as an ordinary man
entertains for his wife
and children
is one's highest duty.

18th October

The universe

is

the common field

where

all the existing minds

can experience

freely their own

individual worlds of

joys and sorrows.

19th October

Both renunciation
of action
and performance
of action
lead to freedom.
But of these,
performance of action
is superior to the
renunciation of action.

20th October

The physical body is the most powerful attraction for the majority of living beings and most of us are aware of nothing nobler and diviner than the body.

21st October

Causation
is the very stuff
of the intellect
and it is, as it were,
the only method
by which the
intellect can
understand and act.

22nd October

Culture
expresses
itself
in
thoughts,
words
and
deeds.

23rd October

Dharma
means not
merely righteousness
or goodness;
it indicates the
essential nature of
anything,
without which
it cannot retain its
independent existence.

24th October

So long as the dreamer
lives the dream,
the Teacher in the dream can
never make
the dreamer understand
that on waking
from the dream,
the dreamer will become
the waker.

25th October

To dissipate our
energies through
the sense organs
is the
vulgar hobby
of the
thoughtless
mortals.

26th October

It is certain
that the faithful
never fall.
Faith,
unswerving faith alone
is the
supreme means
to the
supreme goal.

27th October

Man is
never punished
for
his sins
but
by
his sins.

28th October

Crookedness
in thoughts,
emotions and
general conduct
has a
self-destructive
influence
upon our
personality.

29th October

Objective realization of
God
is only a mental delusion.
God is realized
only subjectively
as a supreme
experience
of consciousness.

30th October

If

by studying the scriptures

one can

become a sannyāsin,

by counting

the king's money,

one must

become a millionaire.

31st October

There is nothing
at any time,
in any circumstance,
to worry over:
"why this to me?"
What
you have is
all His gift to you.
What you do
with what you have
is your gift to Him.

1st November

Only
the
Knower
knows
the
Knower.

2nd November

Every action
motivated
by
egocentric desires
thickens
the veil of ignorance
and permits not
even a single ray of
the essential divinity
to peep through it
to illumine
the life in us.

3rd November

Just as the beauty
of a fruit
is not the last word of
its edibility,
a beautiful action can
be a poisoned act
of cruelty
if the motive behind is
low and vicious.

4th November

Where
there is light,
darkness cannot be.
Where
knowledge has come,
ignorance must
quit.

5th November

The more we identify
with the little 'I' in us,
the more will be our
problems and confusions
in life.
By expanding to identify
with a larger cause,
we shall find our
confusions dwindling
to nothingness.

6th November

If a person speaks ill of
good people,
he is a mean and
despicable creature,
but if somebody hearing those
abusive words,
tries to pay him back in
his own coin,
he is still worse.

7th November

Very often we hear some people complaining that nobody loves me. The world is full of love.

But generally, our hearts are not open for love to gush into us, and the door of your heart ever remains closed.

Nobody other than you can ever throw it open, for the door of your heart cannot be locked from outside; it can be opened only from within.

8th November

Daily prayer
and meditaiton
are all wonderful
therapeutic agencies
in building up
peace and happiness
within
an individual.

9th November

The soul
in its essence is
God.
Soul minus
our egoistic mistake is
God.
God plus
our egoistic mistake
is soul.

10th November

If

the heart

could only

love and serve,

the head

could only

judge and

respect!

11th November

Faults
become
thick
when
love
is
thin.

12th November

In life,

it has always

been observed

that

to solve a

problem

is

to rise

above it.

13th November

To remember
the ever-present Divine
at all times even,
while acting in the world
is the most positive
practice for a seeker
who is striving to evolve.
He will thereby
transform his inner
personality
from its present condition
to a state of
harmony and efficiency.

14th November

That which feels
"I am," this 'I'
is neither mind
nor matter.
It is eternal.
The external things
exist because of the
imaginations of
this 'I'.

15th November

The Lord
is supreme,
dwells
in the hearts of all
and His glory
peeps out
through
equipments.

16th November

When man is threatened
with a sure mishap and
when he knows no remedy
or defense against it,
he, in his desperation,
always turns to prayer.

17th November

Treatises
on
love
are
the
purāṇas.

18th November

The mind control
that leads to acquisition
of siddhis,
and purity of mind
that secures the
vision of God
are different,
according to all
authorities.

19th November

The action
of today
becomes
the destiny
of tomorrow.

20th November

Self
clothed in mind
is the ego in man.
Evolution and change are
all for the
mind and intellect
and not for the
Self.

21st November

The most
marvellous computer
is only
a product
of the
human brain.

22nd November

The culture of the people
must continuously
serve them,
nourishing their
inspiration,
guiding their action and
providing
consolation, comfort,
balance and equanimity
in both their
joys and sorrows.

23rd November

Dharma
comprises those
divine values of life,
by living which
we shall be manifesting
more and more
of the essential
spiritual being
in us.

24th November

To rediscover
ourselves
is to invite
into our lives
the congnition
of a greater intellect
and a
divine Consciousness.

25th November

If enjoyment
is the body,
suffering is its head.
The fewer one's
possessions,
the greater
are one's enjoyment
and freedom.

26th November

Through faith
in Him,
we reach that faith
in us.
What can stop us?
That faith is ours.
Live it!
We must!

27th November

When
I slip outside,
I fall.
When
I slip inside,
I rise.
Without,
I go only to
come down.
Within,
I go only to
rise above.

28th November

Philosophy
without
love
is madness.
Love
without
philosophy
is superstition.

29th November

REFLECT!

<u>Future:</u>

The future is carved out of the present moment. Tomorrow's harvest depends upon today's ploughing and sowing. The past is dead. The future is not yet born. If one is inefficient and unhealthy in the present, he has no reason to hope for a greater future.

30th November

Strive on!
With tireless enthusiasm,
strive on to
reach your goal.
Without a goal,
the best in you
can never
come out to express.

1st December

Everyone with knowledge
exerts, sweats and toils
but only a few succeed in life. They
generally forget
that mind is the doer in us
and the body is but our tool.
Learn to bring your mind
where your hands are working; then
see the results!
Actions become excellent
and success is the tribute
life pays to excellence.

2nd December

By merely
running away
from action,
no one attains
perfection.
Renunciation of life
is not the way
to reach
the highest goal
of evolution.

3rd December

Incompetency
in life
generally springs from
our false
and hasty conclusions
that we are
impotent,
insignificant
and
ineffective.

4th December

Change of vision
is the remedy given by
all Masters of Truth
who have gained
the vision.
Therefore,
keep smiling.
All falls
are a
rise in total.

5th December

To get ourselves
overridden
by life's
circumstances,
is to ensure
disastrous
failures
on all occasions.

6th December

Attachment
is death;
non-attachment
is eternal life.
Life is
a death-long
discipline.

7th December

Interruptions

are

the

spice

of

life.

8th December

A peaceful mind
is a significant condition
of happiness.
An unagitated mind
is itself a proof
against all sorrows.
Sorrow
is nothing but
an agitated condition
of the mind.

9th December

The average man looks up at night, and sees thousands and thousands of twinkiing stars, each different from the other. But a man of wisdom and achievement, perceives the one light, behind the dark dome of the night sky, whose incandesence peeps at us through all the holes in the night-dome! To see the one in many is the casual vision of knowledge. To see the many in the one, is the vision of wisdom.

10th December

The really
poor man
is not the one
who lacks
money,
but who lacks
the joy of the
heart.

11th December

In life to handle yourself,
use your head;
but to handle others,
use your heart.
Be strict
and intelligently critical
about yourself and
your own
weaknesses and follies,
but cushion your words and
attitudes with love.
Love is
the greatest persuasive
power
we know in life.

12th December

Living
the right
values of life
is like
building a dam
across a river.

13th December

Not to do
what
you feel like
doing
is
freedom.

14th December

REFLECT!

Opportunities:

Opportunities in life come
to everyone of us,
almost all the time.
They come in streams,
in hosts
and knock at
our doors.
We are either out or
sleeping in.
Be awake! Be alert!
Be prepared to make
use of them!

15th December

All joys
known to me
in my daily life are
because of me
and
the objects
of my liking.

16th December

To do your job
even if circumstances
are not conducive,
is our gift
to
Him,
who is the sole
Lord
of all circumstances.

17th December

Develop noble
and enduring qualities.
Watch in others for
weaknesses
that you should guard
against in yourself.
Love all. Serve all.
Love creates
and lust destroys
the peace
in the heart of man.

18th December

To give
physically, a show
of morality and ethics,
while mentally
living a shameless life of
low motives and
foul sentiments,
is to be a
self-deluded hypocrite,
according to Gītā.

19th December

Whenever
adorers go,
they are attended by
the Adored,
who saves them from
the perils.

20th December

Food
for the body
is
not so necessary
as prayer for
the soul.

21st December

A word of
sincere sympathy,
a look of love,
a smile of true affection
can give to the recipient
much more than a
heartless cheque,
even if it be for
a fat sum.
So, be truly charitable
in this diviner sense.

22nd December

Continous change
is the nature
of finitude.
It is
this change
that we understand
as death.

23rd December

That dharma which
remains homogeneous,
and unchanging
in all good persons,
and in all good affairs
irrespective of
time and space
alone is
sanātana dharma.

24th December

Humility
is a
strange thing!
The minute
you think
you have
got it,
you have
lost it!

25th December

Love is
a consistent passion
to give,
not a meek persistent
hope to receive.
The only demand
of life is
the privilege
to love all.

26th December

Faith is the
sheet anchor of religion
while intelligence is the
sheet anchor of science.
The two do co-exist
and can and must
co-exist.

27th December

REFLECT!

<u>Friends:</u>

Cultivate friends.
To have a friend is to make
life easier
and richer.
A friend is a present that
you give to yourself.
But you cannot
pick up a friend, nor
purchase a friend.
We cannot compel anyone
to be our friend.
We have to discover a friend.

28th December

Politeness
is the art of
selecting
among
one's real
thoughts.

29th December

Like God,

the vision

of

God

too

is

beyond words.

30th December

Happiness
depends upon
what you can
give,
not on
what you can
get.

31st December

When

the time of

judgement comes,

we shall

not be asked

what we have read

but

what we have done.